by Joyce Markovics

Consultant: Karla Ruiz
Teachers College, Columbia University
New York, New York

BEARPORT
PUBLISHING

New York, New York

Credits

Cover, © wavebreakmedia/Shutterstock and © Jess Kraft/Shutterstock; TOC, © Michaelpuche/Shutterstock; 4, © Jess Kraft/Shutterstock; 5L, © Francisco J Ramos Gallego/Shutterstock; 5R, © Eduardo Rivero/Shutterstock; 7, © Gary C. Tognoni/Shutterstock.com; 8–9, © Jess Kraft/Shutterstock; 8B, © Jess Kraft/Shutterstock; 9T, COLPRENSA Xinhua News Agency/Newscom; 10L, © Dirk Ercken/Shutterstock; 10R, © nattanan726/Shutterstock; 11, © Rafal Cichawa/iStock; 11B, © Mikadun/Shutterstock; 12–13, © Jane Sweeney/JAI/Corbis; 12L, © Videowokart/Shutterstock; 13T, © M Rutherford/Shutterstock; 14–15, © Andresr/Shutterstock; 15L, © Fotos593/Shutterstock; 16, © javarman/Shutterstock; 17L, © DC_Colombia/iStock; 17R, © PRISMA ARCHIVO/Alamy; 18, © javarman/Shutterstock; 19, © Horizons WWP/Alamy; 20–21, © Gary C. Tognoni/Shutterstock; 22–23, © Kike Calvo/National Geographic Creative/Corbis; 24, © Prometheus72/Shutterstock; 25, © Lipskiy/Shutterstock; 26, © Juanmonino/iStock; 27, © almondd/Shutterstock; 28, © AGIF/Shutterstock; 29, © AGIF/Shutterstock; 30L, © JackF/iStock; 30TR, © Asaf Eliason/Shutterstock; 30BR, © ppart/Shutterstock; 31(T to B), © javarman/Shutterstock, © Jess Kraft/Shutterstock, © Gary C. Tognoni/Shutterstock, © DC_Apeture/Shutterstock, and © amenic181/Shutterstock; 32, © Bocman1973/Shutterstock.

Publisher: Kenn Goin
Senior Editor: Joyce Tavolacci
Creative Director: Spencer Brinker
Design: Debrah Kaiser
Photo Researcher: Olympia Shannon

Library of Congress Cataloging-in-Publication Data

Markovics, Joyce.
  Colombia / by Joyce Markovics.
    pages cm. — (Countries we come from)
  Includes bibliographical references and index.
  Audience: Ages 4–7.
  ISBN 978-1-943553-34-1 (library binding) — ISBN 1-943553-34-3 (library binding)
  1. Colombia—Juvenile literature. I. Title.
  F2258.5.M38 2015
  986.1—dc23
                              2015029757

For more information, write to Bearport Publishing Company, Inc., 45 West 21st Street, Suite 3B, New York, New York 10010. Printed in the United States of America.

10 9 8 7 6 5 4 3 2 1

Contents

This Is Colombia...... 4

Fast Facts.................30

Glossary 31

Index 32

Read More 32

Learn More Online 32

About the Author 32

This Is Colombia

Beautiful

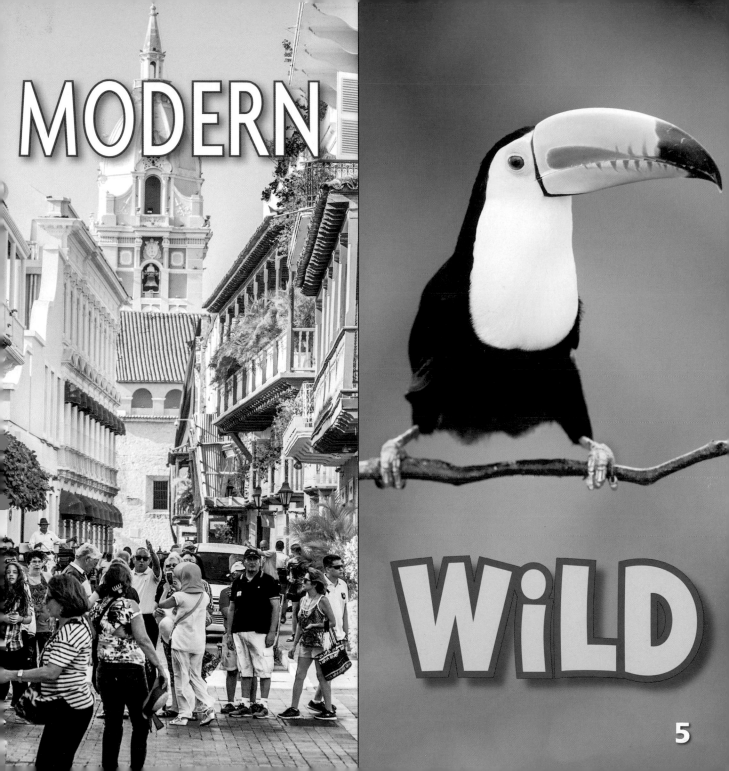

MODERN

WiLD

Colombia is a large country in South America.

More than 46 million people live there.

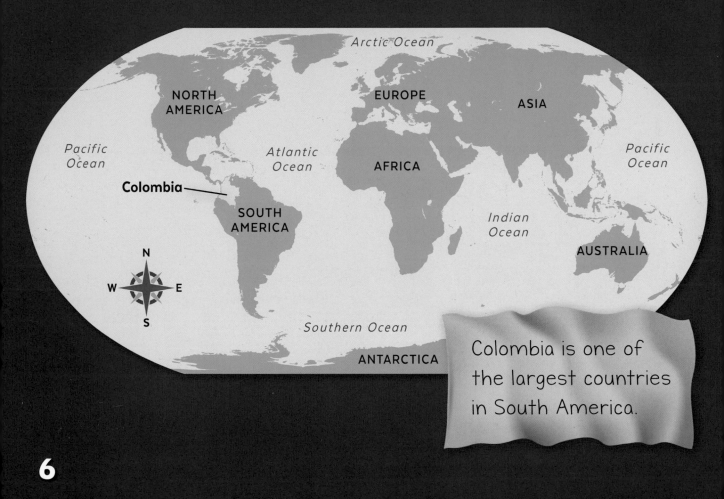

Colombia is one of the largest countries in South America.

Deserts, beaches, and mountains—Colombia has it all.

desert

There are more than 300 beaches in Colombia.

The country even has
snow-covered volcanoes!

Thick, wet forests cover almost half the country.

Sloths hang upside-down from trees.

Colorful frogs rest on large leaves.

two-toed sloth

poison dart frog

Spotted jaguars
also live in
Colombia's forests.

The **soil** in Colombia is dark and rich.

Farmers grow coffee plants in it.

Colombian coffee is very tasty.

It's famous around the world!

coffee beans

a farmer picking coffee beans

Colombian farmers also grow lots of bananas.

The biggest city in Colombia is Bogotá.

It's nestled in the Andes Mountains.

Bogotá is the country's **capital**.

Andes Mountains

People have been living in Colombia for thousands of years.

They settled throughout the country.

They left **artifacts** behind.

a gold mask found in Colombia that's more than 1,000 years old

a stone figure made by people who lived in Colombia long ago

In 1500, the Spanish came to Colombia. They ruled for hundreds of years.

Today, most Colombians speak Spanish.

This is how you say *hello* in Spanish:

Hola (OH-lah)

This is how you say *please*:

Por favor (PORE fah-VORE)

Ninety–nine percent of Colombians speak Spanish. Other people speak **native** languages.

There are lots of colorful **festivals** in Colombia.

One of the biggest is Barranquilla's Carnival.

People wear fancy costumes.

They sing and dance in the streets.

Barranquilla is a city in northern Colombia.

Carolina Cruz
Modelo

21

Colombia is known for a special kind of dance.

It's called salsa.

Salsa dancers move their feet quickly.

They step forward, backward, and spin around.

Cali is a Colombian city. It's known as the World's Salsa Capital.

Many well-known artists are from Colombia.

Fernando Botero is one of the most famous.

Fernando Botero

Botero was born in 1932 in Medellín, Colombia.

He paints and sculpts
chubby animals and people.

What are some popular foods in Colombia?

People enjoy crisp corn cakes called arepas (ah-RAY-pahs).

Arepas are often stuffed with cheese or eggs.

Colombians also eat a hearty soup called Ajiaco (ah-hee-AH-koh).

It's made with potatoes, corn, and chicken.

What else do Colombians enjoy?

Soccer!

It's the most popular sport in the country.

Fans cheer for their favorite teams!

Colombians call soccer "fútbol" (FOOT–bole).

Fast Facts

Capital city: Bogotá

Population of Colombia: More than 46 million

Main language: Spanish

Money: Colombian peso

Major religion: Roman Catholic

Neighboring countries include: Panama, Venezuela, Brazil, Peru, and Ecuador

Cool Fact: The national animal of Colombia is the Andean Condor. This huge bird has a wingspan of 10 feet (3 m)!

artifacts (ART-uh-fakts) objects of historical interest that were made by people

capital (KAP-uh-tuhl) a city where a country's government is based

festivals (FESS-tuh-vuhlz) celebrations or holidays

native (NAY-tiv) belonging to a particular place

soil (SOYL) dirt or earth in which plants grow

31

Index

animals 10–11, 30
art 24–25
capital 14–15
cities 14–15, 20–21, 23

dance 22–23
food 12–13, 26–27
festivals 7, 20–21
history 16–17

land 8–9, 10–11, 14
language 18, 30
population 6, 30
sports 28–29

Read More

Blackford, Cheryl. *Colombia (Country Explorers).* Minneapolis, MN: Lerner (2011).

Yomtov, Nel. *Colombia (Enchantment of the World).* New York: Scholastic (2014).

Learn More Online

To learn more about Colombia, visit
www.bearportpublishing.com/CountriesWeComeFrom

About the Author

Joyce Markovics is a writer from New York who longs to visit South America with her Colombian neighbor and friend, Natalia.